Raintree Rhymers

Book Two

The Grand Old Duke of York
One, Two, Three, Four, Five
Diddle, Diddle, Dumpling
I See the Moon

Raintree Childrens Books

Text copyright © 1986 Raintree Publishers Inc.

Illustrations copyright © 1981 Ginn and Company Ltd.

Library of Congress Number: 85-12429

Library of Congress Cataloging in Publication Data
Main entry under title:
  Raintree rhymers.

  Summary: Four books include familiar nursery rhymes
such as "Humpty Dumpty," "Little Miss Muffet," and
"Rain, Rain, Go Away," accompanied by activity pages
with rhyming exercises for beginning readers.
  1. Nursery rhymes.   2. Children's poetry.
[1. Nursery rhymes]
PZ8.3.R145   1985   398′.8   85-12429

ISBN 0-8172-2452-1 (lib. bdg.)
ISBN 0-8172-2457-2 (softcover)

Oh, the grand old Duke of York,

He had ten thousand men.

He marched them up
To the top of the hill,

And he marched them down again!

And when they were up,
They were up.

And when they were down,
They were down.

And when they were
Only half way up,

They were neither up nor down.

Oh, the grand old Duke of York,

He had ten thousand men.

He marched them up

To the top of the hill,

And he marched them down again!

And when they were up,

They were up.

And when they were down,

They were down.

And when they were

Only half way up,

They were neither up nor down.

It Sounds Like . . .

Words that rhyme, sound alike, like *cork, pork, York.*
Think of words that sound like **down, grand,** and **York.**
These three poems will help you.

1. To think of a word
   That sounds like **down,**
   Think of a king
   Who is wearing a _____ .

2. To think of a word
   That sounds like **grand,**
   Think of the beach
   And walking on _____ .

3. To think of a word
   That sounds like **York,**
   Think of eating
   Your cake with a _____ .

Write a Poem

Now, finish these three poems. Choose a word for each blank. Your word should sound like the word in capital letters.

1. The Duke of York had a strong WILL.
   He marched his men right up the _____ .

2. These soldiers are a good looking CREW,
   With their coats of red and hats of _____ .

3. Straight up the hill, the duke led his FORCE,
   But the men were marching and he had a _____ .

One, two, three, four, five,
I caught a fish alive.

Six, seven, eight, nine, ten,
I let it go again.

Why did you let it go?

Because it bit my finger so.

Which finger did it bite?

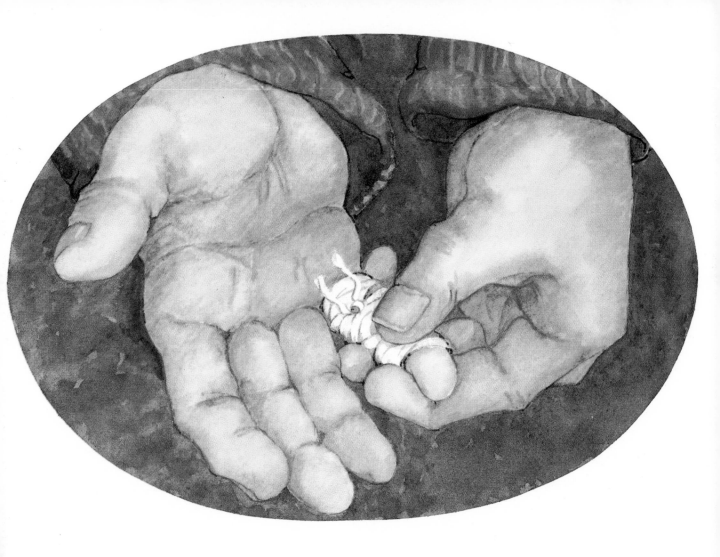

This little finger on the right.

FISH·SHOP

19

One, two, three, four, five,

I caught a fish alive.

Six, seven, eight, nine, ten,

I let it go again.

Why did you let it go?

Because it bit my finger so.

Which finger did it bite?

This little finger on the right.

It Sounds Like . . .

Words that rhyme, sound alike, like *fish*, *wish*, *dish*. Think of words that sound like **right, bite,** and **caught.** These three poems will help you.

1. To think of a word
   That sounds like **right,**
   Think of when the sun goes down,
   And day turns into _____ .

2. To think of a word
   That sounds like **bite,**
   Think of early morning,
   When it's getting _____ .

3. To think of a word
   That sounds like **caught,**
   Think of your school
   And the things you were _____ .

Write a Poem

Now, finish these three poems. Choose a word for each blank. Your word should sound like the word in capital letters.

1. Fishing is a lot of FUN,
Even if you only catch _____ .

2. One fish each for Mom and Dad and ME.
Let's see. That means I have to catch _____ .

3. I have my pole and also the BAIT.
Who knows? I may catch seven or _____ .

Diddle, diddle, dumpling

My son John

Went to bed with his trousers on.

One shoe off
And one shoe on.

Diddle, diddle, dumpling

My son John.

I see the moon.

The moon sees me.

God bless the moon,

And God bless me.
Good night.

Diddle, diddle, dumpling
My son John
Went to bed with his trousers on.
One shoe off
And one shoe on.
Diddle, diddle, dumpling
My son John.

I see the moon.
The moon sees me.
God bless the moon,
And God bless me.
Good night.

It Sounds Like . . .

Words that rhyme, sound alike, like *noon, soon, tune.*
Think of words that sound like **son, see,** and **good.**
These three poems will help you.

1. To think of a word
   That sounds like **son,**
   Think of a game you have played,
   And how you lost or _____ .

2. To think of a word
   That sounds like **see,**
   Think first of you
   And then of _____ .

3. To think of a word
   That sounds like **good,**
   Think of a tall, tall tree,
   Which is made of _____ .

Write a Poem

Now, finish these three poems. Choose a word for each blank. Your word should sound like the word in capital letters.

1. I look at the colors of my BED.
Then I name them . . . green, blue, _____ .

2. You can always see the sun at NOON.
But at night when you look, you see the _____ .

3. Tucked into my bed at NIGHT,
I hug my teddy bear real _____ .